Women in Profile

Athletes

Leslie Strudwick

Crabtree Publishing Company

Dedication

This series is dedicated to every woman who has followed her dreams and to every young girl who hopes to do the same. While overcoming great odds and often oppression, the remarkable women in this series have triumphed in their fields. Their dedication, hard work, and excellence can serve as an inspiration to all—young and old, male and female. Women in Profile is both an acknowledgment of and a tribute to these great women.

Project Coordinator
Leslie Strudwick
Crabtree Editor
Virginia Mainprize
Editing and Proofreading
Carlotta Lemieux
Alana Luft
Krista McLuskey
Design
Warren Clark

Published by Crabtree Publishing Company

350 Fifth Avenue, Suite 3308
New York, NY
USA 10018

360 York Road, R.R. 4
Niagara-on-the-Lake
Ontario, Canada
L0S 1J0

Cataloging-in-Publication Data

Strudwick, Leslie. 1970–
    Athletes / Leslie Strudwick.
        p. cm. — (Women in profile)
    Includes bibliographical references (p.) and index.
    Summary: Chronicles the lives and achievements of talented women athletes, including speed skater Bonnie Blair, gymnast Nadia Comaneci, and track athlete Wilma Rudolph.
    ISBN 0-7787-0015-1. — ISBN 0-7787-0037-2 (pbk.)
    1. Athletes—Biography—Juvenile literature. 2. Women athletes—Biography—Juvenile literature. [1. Athletes. 2. Women—Biography.] I. Title. II. Series.
GV697.A1S78   1999
796'.082'0922—dc21
[b]
                                    98–40519
                                            CIP
                                            AC

Photograph Credits
Every reasonable effort has been made to trace ownership and to obtain permission to reprint copyright material. The publishers would be pleased to have any errors or omissions brought to their attention so that they may be corrected in subsequent printings.

Agence France Presse/Corbis-Bettmann: page 42 (Jean Loup Gautreau); Archive Photos: cover, pages 10, 11, 14, 20, 22, 23, 24, 29, 32, 36, 38, 41, 45; Canapress Photo Service: pages 9, 17, 43, 44; Corbis-Bettmann: page 19; Image Works: pages 21, 35; Photofest: pages 8, 18, 40; Reuters/Corbis-Bettmann: pages 6 (Thomas Szlukovenyi), 28 (Mike Blake); Courtesy of the Salk Institute for Biological Sciences: page 31; Tennessee State University: page 33; UPI/Corbis-Bettmann: pages 12, 15, 16, 26, 27, 30, 34, 37, 39.

Contents

Athletes

Women have not always been allowed to compete in athletic events. When the first modern Olympic Games were held in 1896, all the **competitors** were men. This changed only four years later at the Olympic Games held in Paris, France. Out of 1,330 competitors, only 12 were women. It was not many, but it was a start.

Today, women from all around the world compete in athletic events, in most cases against other women. There are some sports, such as horse racing, in which women compete directly with men, and the number of these events is growing. Women athletes are gaining more respect with every passing year. They train, work, and play just as hard as male athletes, and their competitions are just as exciting.

The women in this book all have different backgrounds and talents, but they realized it took more than talent to reach the top. Each woman worked very hard to achieve the **status** she gained in her sport.

There are thousands of women athletes across the globe, far too many to be featured in a single book. The women in this book span a number of sports and a variety of skills. Some compete in sports that are more common for women, while others have gone off the beaten path. They have all excelled through hard work and determination to become the best athletes they could possibly be.

"I don't really think too much about the pressure ... I take each weekend or competition one at a time."

Bonnie Blair

American Speed Skater

Early Years

Every Wednesday was speed-skating night in the Blair household. The Wednesday night that Bonnie Blair was born was no exception. Her father was at the skating rink with the other Blair children while Eleanor Blair was giving birth to Bonnie in the hospital. Her arrival was announced over the loudspeaker at the rink, "Another speed skater has been born to the Blair family." One might say that Bonnie Blair was born to speed skate.

Once Bonnie was old enough to walk, her older brothers and sisters could not wait to get her skating. They took the smallest pair of skates they could find and slipped them on right over her shoes! All it took was one little push, and two-year-old Bonnie was skating.

BACKGROUNDER

History of Skating

Remains of old skates, dating from as far back as 50 B.C., have been found in England. These early skates had leather soles, and the blades were made from polished animal bones. It was not until over one thousand years later that ice skating, as a form of recreation, began in England. Before then, skates with iron blades were used for quick winter travel. The skates we have today were developed by E.W. Bushnell in 1850 in Philadelphia, Pennsylvania. The blades are made from steel rather than iron.

Bonnie was on skates before she was three years old.

Developing Skills

Two years after Bonnie first put on skates, she began to enter races. Some of the racing meets were very long. Bonnie could often be found on her mother's lap taking a nap. Sometimes, she slept right through her Tiny Tots races!

Bonnie loved going to the skating rink. In winter, the Blair family spent most weekends at skating rinks across the midwestern United States. It was not long before Bonnie was as good a racer as her older brothers and sisters. By the age of seven, she was racing in the Illinois State Championships.

During these early years, Bonnie raced on hockey rinks in speed-skating events, called pack skating. Pack racers gather on the ice, and all race against each other at the same time. In order to win, racers need a quick start and have to elbow their way to the front of the pack. This style of racing helped Bonnie develop her strong starts. One reporter referred to Bonnie's starts as "turbo-charged."

Bonnie always ate a peanut butter and jelly sandwich before each competition. This tradition started when she was very young, and she continued it for luck.

Bonnie's racing skills developed quickly, and she took home a number of trophies. She won her first National Indoor Speed-Skating title when she was only ten years old.

Bonnie's father, Charlie, spent hours at the rink, helping out at his children's practices and races. He was proud of all his children, but he took note of Bonnie's special talent and had high hopes for her. "She's going to skate in the Olympics, and she's going to win a gold medal," he proudly stated. Bonnie had not even considered this possibility before. She loved to be on the ice and race, but going all the way to the Olympics? That would take a lot of work.

"It was my dad's dream that I'd be in the Olympics before it was ever my dream."

Bonnie began to think seriously about the Olympics when Canadian speed skater Cathy Priestner saw her race. Cathy had won at the Olympics and thought Bonnie could win, too. The two started training together, and Bonnie soon thought the idea of racing in the Olympics sounded better and better.

In 1982, Bonnie went to Europe to train with some of the best speed skaters in the world.

BACKGROUNDER

The Olympic Winter Games

The Winter Olympics are held in January or February every four years. They usually last about twelve days. For a sport to be included in the Games, it must be very popular in at least twenty-five countries on two continents. The host city of the Winter Games must have an outdoor stadium where the opening ceremony is held. The speed-skating races are often held in this stadium as well, unless the city has an indoor skating oval.

Accomplishments

With Cathy's help, Bonnie went to the U.S. Olympic trials in 1980. She was just fifteen and one of the youngest skaters there. Bonnie did not **qualify** for the **Olympic team**, but she did make up her mind that she would get on the team one day.

When Bonnie returned home to Champaign, Illinois, she worked harder than ever. She started lifting weights to build up her strength. She drove nine hours every weekend to train at the indoor speed-skating rink in Milwaukee. The rink in Milwaukee was an Olympic rink, a 400-meter track. The skaters there competed in long-track races. Long track is when just two skaters race at a time. Officials note the times taken by each skater, and they declare a winner after everyone has raced.

Once Bonnie was finished high school, she wanted to move to Milwaukee to train full time. This move was expensive, and the Blair family could not afford it. In order to help Bonnie reach the Olympics, the Champaign Police Force raised the $7,000 she needed. They collected some of the money by selling bumper stickers calling Bonnie "Champaign Policemen's Favorite Speeder."

"She's got an incredible head for competition, she always races well."
Olympic teammate Dan Jansen

Champaign's hometown spirit and Bonnie's hard work paid off. Bonnie went to her first Olympic meet in 1984. Although she did not win, it taught her how to prepare for the next Olympics.

The 1988 Olympics were held in Calgary, Canada. Bonnie had just appeared on the cover of *Life* magazine and was called "Best Bet for U.S. Gold." She certainly lived up to these expectations. She won a gold medal in the 500-meter race, and she also won a bronze in the 1,000-meter race.

These are not the only Olympic medals Bonnie has won. She went on to win four more Olympic gold medals in 1992 and 1994. These wins, along with a number of National and World Championships, have made Bonnie Blair perhaps the best female speed skater in history.

Quick Notes

- A group of Bonnie's friends and relatives followed her to the Olympic Games in 1988, 1992, and 1994. They were nicknamed the Blair Bunch and were often the loudest cheering section in the stands.

- Bonnie dedicated her first gold medal to her brother Rob. He had just been diagnosed with a brain tumor. She dedicated her second gold medal to her dad, who had died from cancer.

- Bonnie often received letters in the mail addressed only to "Bonnie Blair, Olympic Gold Medalist." The envelopes had no address or stamp.

In Bonnie's hometown of Champaign, there is a road named after her. It is called Bonnie Blair Drive.

"Yes, I had confidence, I was sure I would win. Gymnastics requires grace above all, but also courage. Then you must stick to it and work hard."

Nadia Comaneci

Romanian Gymnast

Early Years

Nadia was born in Onesti, a factory town in the mountains of Romania. Romania has many old castles, one of which is said to have belonged to Count Dracula! That was long before Nadia's time.

Nadia and her family lived in a small apartment. She was a lively child who loved to run and jump. She loved jumping so much that she broke four of her family's couches by jumping on them so often that the springs snapped.

There was a sports school in Onesti where the country's women gymnasts trained. One day, the gymnastics coach Bela Karolyi visited Nadia's school. He saw Nadia and another girl pretending to be gymnasts during recess, and he started to go over to talk to them. Just then the bell rang, and Nadia and her friend rushed into the school. Bela did not want to leave until he found the two girls. He went from class to class looking for them. Each time he asked, "Who loves gymnastics here?" In the third room, two girls jumped up saying, "We do, we do!" Bela had found the two girls he was looking for, one of whom was Nadia Comaneci.

Backgrounder

Romania

Romania is a **communist** country in Eastern Europe. Its name means land of the Romans. The capital city is called Bucharest. Romania was ruled by a communist dictator until 1990. During that time, freedoms were greatly restricted. If people wanted to move away from Romania, they had to **defect**.

Developing Skills

O nce Bela found Nadia, he took her to his gym for a test. Each child who wanted to train with Bela had to pass this test. She was asked to run a fifteen-meter sprint, do a long jump, and walk on the balance beam. The balance beam was the most important part of the test. If the children were afraid of the beam, Bela sent them home. The beam was 4 feet (1.2 meters) above the floor and only 4 inches (10 centimeters) wide. It did not frighten Nadia. She walked across it as if she was walking along the sidewalk.

Nadia passed the test with flying colors. Bela asked her parents if they would let her train at his gym. Although she was only six years old, they agreed.

"She has three qualities. The physical qualities—strength, speed, agility. The intellectual qualities—intelligence and the power to concentrate. And above everything, Nadia has courage."

Bela Karolyi

Bela said Nadia was the perfect pupil. "She knew no fear." She trained six days a week, four hours a day. Nadia was usually the first person to arrive in the morning and the first to start warming up for her workout. She practiced exercises over and over again without complaining and never seemed to tire.

Nadia trained every day except Sunday.

Within a year, Nadia was ready for her first competition. She entered the Romanian National Junior Gymnastics Championship. She was the youngest **competitor** and placed thirteenth. This was quite good for such a young girl, but Bela knew she could do better. He gave her a little doll for good luck and told her "never to finish thirteenth again." She never did.

The next year, Nadia returned to the National Junior Championship with her little doll. She did not place thirteenth that year—she placed first. She was only eight years old.

The year 1971 was an important one for Nadia. She became a member of the Romanian gymnastics team. She also won the national overall gymnastics title for her age group. The same year, she traveled to Bulgaria, a neighboring country, to compete in the Friendship Cup Meet. This was the first time Nadia had competed against gymnasts outside Romania. She came away with two gold medals. The following year, she won the National Junior Championship for a third time, and she left the Friendship Cup Meet with three gold medals.

Backgrounder

Gymnastics

Gymnastic routines are performed on various types of **apparatuses**. Men and women compete separately. In women's gymnastics, there are four different events: the side horse vault, the uneven parallel bars, the balance beam, and the floor exercise. In **international** competitions, women gymnasts must compete in each event. For each event, judges award a score. The scoring is between 1 and 10—10 being perfect.

Nadia performs a back handspring during a routine on the balance beam.

Quick Notes

- **With the doll he gave her for good luck, Bela started Nadia's doll collection. She began collecting dolls from every place she visited. By the time she was fourteen, she had over two hundred.**

- **Nadia was awarded the Hero of Socialist Labor after her performance at the 1976 Olympics. It was the highest honor in her country. She was the youngest woman ever to receive it.**

- **Nadia donated $120,000 to the Romanian gymnastics team in 1994.**

Accomplishments

I n 1975, Nadia was old enough to compete as a senior. She entered the European Championships and won one silver and four gold medals. One of the gold medals was for the all-round competition. Nadia was the youngest girl ever to have won it.

With Nadia's excellent performances in Europe and at the pre-Olympic meets in the United States and Canada, she was ready for the big event. Ever since Nadia had started gymnastics, she had dreamed of going to the Olympic Games. In 1976, when she was just fourteen years old, she got her chance.

The Games were held in Montreal, Canada. The first event in gymnastics, Nadia's favorite, was the uneven parallel bars. When it was her turn, Nadia burst onto the bars with determination and force that seemed too strong for such a small girl. She went through her steps with such ease that she looked as if she were "swimming in an ocean of air," as one announcer put it. When she finished her routine, she leapt off the bars and onto the floor with the same force.

In 1976, Nadia scored a perfect 10 on the balance beam and on the uneven parallel bars.

The crowd was silent, waiting to see what her score would be. Then the scoreboard flashed a 1.00. The crowd still sat in silence, not knowing what the score meant. Nadia could not have received only 1 out of 10 points. Suddenly, everyone realized that the 1.00 was actually a 10. They roared and cheered. No one had ever received a score of 10 in an Olympic competition. The scoreboard did not have enough room to display four digits. That is why the judges had to put up 1.00.

This perfect score was not the only one for Nadia at the 1976 Olympic Games. She went on to receive the score of 10 seven more times! Her Olympic dream had come true. She won three gold medals, a silver, and a bronze.

Nadia went back to the Olympics in 1980 in Moscow, the capital of the Soviet Union. She won two gold and two silver medals. Nadia also went to the Olympics in 1984, but not as a competitor. This time she went as the coach of the Romanian gymnastics team. Nadia had become the person who went to schools looking for future gymnasts like herself.

BACKGROUNDER

Leaving Romania

After Bela and his wife Marta defected from Romania in 1981, Nadia began to think about moving to another country. The Romanian government watched her carefully because they thought that she too might defect. She was no longer allowed to travel outside the country or to judge international competitions. In 1989, Nadia escaped from Romania, crossing the border in the middle of the night. She left behind her family, her medals, and everything she owned. She moved to the United States and now operates a gymnastics school in Oklahoma with her husband, Bart Conner, another Olympic champion.

Nadia and her husband, Bart Conner, are both Olympic medal winners.

KEY EVENTS

1923 Wins her first Norwegian skating championship

1924 Places last at the Olympic Games

1927 Wins her first of ten consecutive World Championships

1928 Wins her first of nine consecutive European Championships

1928, 1932, 1936 Wins Olympic gold medals

1936 Turns professional and starts her own touring ice show

1937 Stars in her first movie, *One in a Million*

1982 Is inducted into the International Women's Sports Hall of Fame

"I want to go into pictures and I want to do well. I want to do with skates what Fred Astaire is doing with dancing. No one has ever done it in the movies, and I want to."

Sonja Henie

Norwegian Figure Skater

Early Years

Sonja was born in Oslo, Norway, into a very wealthy family. Her father was the first person in Oslo to own an automobile, and he later had his own private airplane.

Sonja was a bubbly and happy child, and her parents let her do almost anything she wanted. What Sonja wanted to do most was play dress-up and dance. She often put on dancing shows for her dance teacher and family. Sonja loved attention.

Sonja also loved her brother, Leif, but she was a little jealous of him. Because he was five years older, he could go out skating. Sonja wanted to go and skate too. One day, she followed Leif to hockey practice, carrying an old pair of skates. She begged him to teach her to skate. Sonja learned quickly, and soon she entered a race for children. At only five years old, she won the race. Her prize was a little silver paper cutter. Sonja loved this prize and kept it with her always for good luck.

BACKGROUNDER

Norway

Norway is a narrow country in northern Europe. It neighbors three other Scandinavian countries: Sweden, Denmark, and Finland. The northern part of Norway is above the Arctic Circle. Because of this, there are some weeks in summer when the sun shines twenty-four hours a day. Norway is called the Land of the Midnight Sun.

"Brilliant winter days always went to my head anyway, and when I could add speed that I made myself to the natural whip of the wind, I wanted never to go indoors."

Sonja with her brother, Lief.

BACKGROUNDER

Sonja's Training

Once Sonja decided to be a skater, she worked hard to be the best one in the world. Most days, she started at 6:00 A.M. with a three-hour training session. Her meals were strictly controlled, only nutritious food at set times each day. Sonja was tutored in her school subjects only when they could be fitted in with her training schedule. She skated for hours in the afternoon as well. Dance lessons were also a part of her daily training.

Developing Skills

Although dancing had been Sonja's first love, skating soon took its place. She loved speed, and she could only enjoy speed when she had skates on her feet.

Leif was a patient teacher. He taught Sonja how to go fast, and he taught her how to fall so she would not hurt herself. Sonja loved skating so much that she even practiced at home without her skates. Skimming across the floor, she pretended to go through the motions of gliding on the ice. Each morning, Sonja was at the skating rink waiting for it to open, and she often forgot to go home for supper when she went to the rink after school.

When Sonja was six years old, a member of a private club noticed her. Hjordis Olsen offered to teach little Sonja. Soon, she was Hjordis's best student. Even at a young age, Sonja aimed for perfection. She would practice a figure over and over until she could do it ten times in a row and leave only one line in the ice.

Sonja learned ballet as well as skating.

When Sonja was eight, she entered a junior competition. It was in class C, for less-experienced skaters. Sonja won easily. In fact, she did so well that she was allowed to skip four levels and compete on a Senior A level. Senior A meant the National Championships. Sonja entered them the following year, and won. At only nine years old, Sonja was Norway's national ice-skating champion. At the awards ceremony, the head of the national championship committee seemed able to look into the future. He said, "Miss Henie is on her way to becoming the greatest ice-skating champion in history."

"Superstitions give one courage that is like a fake boost. Maybe the paper cutter saw me through that first world championship event. No skating trophy has ever meant as much to me as that first simple one."

With Sonja's success in skating, her family life changed. Everyone was dedicated to making Sonja the best. Her mother rearranged meals and other events in the household to fit with Sonja's needs. Her father canceled his business trips if they interfered with Sonja's schedule.

As Norway's champion, Sonja went to the Olympic Games in 1924 in Chamonix, France. Sonja was a good skater for her age, but she was still not good enough to compete with the best in the world. She came in eighth and last. Although she was disappointed, she vowed to do better next time.

Quick Notes

- In Oslo, there is a museum dedicated to Sonja. It holds many of the 1,470 trophies she won throughout her career. One of the trophies is the little silver paper cutter she won when she was five.

- Sonja never missed or canceled a performance.

- Sonja was married three times.

- In 1938, Sonja's Hollywood Ice Revue was considered the greatest box office attraction in the world.

"[Skating] is not simply a sport, but an art."

Accomplishments

S onja returned to Norway and practiced more than ever. She did not want to lose again. Sonja upgraded her style, her jumps, and her performances. She also went back to her ballet lessons. She brought many of the movements she learned in ballet to her skating. Sonja was the first person to bring these two skills together. She wanted to put on more of a show for her audience. She had special costumes made for her. She shortened her skirts and added colors and trim.

Sonja won the Norwegian National Championship again in 1925 and 1926. It was announced that the World Championship was going to be held in Oslo, the capital of Norway, in 1927. Some people thought that Sonja should not compete. After all, she had not done well in 1924 when competing with skaters from other countries. Sonja's father fought hard to make sure his daughter could enter. He thought it would be a disgrace for Norway if their own champion did not compete. Sonja certainly did not disgrace her country. Much to everyone's surprise, she won, the youngest person ever to do so. She was only fourteen years old.

This World Championship was not the only one Sonja won. She continued to win the championship for the next nine years! In between these contests, Sonja represented Norway in the Olympic Games in 1928, 1932, and 1936. Each time, she won the gold medal.

In 1936, Sonja retired from **amateur** competition. She turned **professional** and began touring with her own ice show. She moved to Hollywood and became a movie star, performing in over a dozen movies. During the late 1930s and the early 1940s, Sonja was one of the main reasons people went to the movies. If they could not see her skate in person, they wanted to see her on the screen.

Sonja Henie became known as the "First Lady of the Ice." She is **credited** with turning figure skating into the popular sport it has become today. No skater has come close to breaking the records Sonja set.

BACKGROUNDER

The Hollywood Years

Sonja had been admired as a skater for years. Once she turned professional, the public grew to love her. Her traveling ice show sold out in almost every city. Sonja earned a very good salary for skating in the ice shows. When she started skating in movies, she earned even more. She was the highest-paid female star during her peak in Hollywood. By the age of twenty-six, she had become a millionaire.

Sonja loved making money, and she loved all the things it could buy. When a burglar broke into her hotel room one night and stole two fur coats, Sonja chased him in her nightgown. Sonja was also very generous. She often let groups of orphans come to her shows for free. She gave her backup skaters cashmere sweaters and other expensive gifts.

Sonja was the star in twelve movies.

"Sports are good for young women. It's good to compete, good to run, good to sweat, good to get dirty, good to feel tired and healthy and refreshed."

Martina Navratilova

Czechoslovakian Tennis Player

Early Years

It is no surprise that Martina Navratilova is a great athlete. She comes from a family of Czechoslovakian athletes. Her father was a ski patrolman. Her mother was an **amateur** tennis champion who later taught ski lessons. Her grandmother also had been a tennis champion. But it was Martina's stepfather, Mirek, who taught Martina to play tennis.

Martina used to take her grandmother's old tennis racket and hit tennis balls against the wall while waiting for her mother and stepfather at their tennis club. Martina did this for months. Then one day, Mirek took her onto the tennis court for her first lesson. She was six years old.

Mirek noticed Martina's talent from the start. She was so eager to learn, and she always followed his directions. If she missed a ball, she just tried harder. Mirek loved to teach his stepdaughter, and Martina has always been grateful. Martina later said, "If he had a dollar for every hour he spent with me, my stepfather would be a millionaire. He loved me so much."

"I never had to be pushed. I loved the game...."

BACKGROUNDER

Czechoslovakia

Czechoslovakia was a country in Central Europe bordered by Germany, Poland, Austria, and Hungary. After World War II, the country was led by a **communist** government. The government controlled all the businesses, industries, farms, churches, and schools. In 1968, the Soviet Union invaded Czechoslovakia and held control until 1989. In 1992, Czechoslovakia split into two countries: the Czech Republic and Slovakia. Prague is the capital of the Czech Republic.

Developing Skills

S oon, Martina was good enough to play in **tournaments**. She entered her first one when she was eight years old. The officials running the tournament did not want Martina to play. They thought she was not strong enough. Martina surprised them by making it to the semifinals.

> "The moment I stepped onto that crunchy red clay, felt the grit under my sneakers, felt the joy of smacking the ball over the net, I knew I was in the right place."

Before long, Martina was playing so well that Mirek had nothing more to teach her. He got her a try-out with George Parma, the coach of the Czech Tennis Federation. George was the coach at Prague's only public club with indoor courts. Soon, Martina was taking the train every day to practice with George Parma. With this new coaching, she entered more and more tournaments. She won many of her matches and soon made the national team.

With the national team, Martina got to travel to West Germany. This was her first trip outside Czechoslovakia. Under the communist government, Czechoslovakians were not allowed to leave the country whenever they wanted. Martina loved what she saw in West Germany. Everyone seemed to have plenty of money, and all the houses had running water. People were free to lead the lives they chose and to say what they pleased about the government. This was not the case in Czechoslovakia. Martina became unhappy with her country and wanted to leave.

When Martina was not playing tennis, she liked to play soccer and hockey.

Despite this unhappiness, Martina continued to play for the Tennis Federation. She also continued to improve as a tennis player. At fourteen, she won her first national title in the fourteen-and-under division. Two years later, she won the first of her three National Women's Championships.

In the summer of 1973, Martina was given permission to go to the United States to compete. Martina loved the United States, especially its fast food. She quickly put on weight. Because of this extra weight, Martina did not win as many matches as she had hoped. She returned to the United States again in 1974 and won more matches this time. She was named Rookie of the Year by *Tennis* magazine.

In 1975, Martina was tired of the Czechoslovakian government telling her where and when she could play tennis. During her trip to the United States that year, she decided to **defect**. She knew she would not be able to go home again. Although this was a difficult decision, she felt it was the best one for her.

Against the wishes of the Czechoslovakian communist government, Martina moved to the United States when she was eighteen.

BACKGROUNDER

Tennis

Tennis was developed during the 1100s or 1200s in France. It began with two players hitting a ball back and forth over a net with the palm of their hand. The modern version of tennis was created in England by Major Walter Clopton Wingfield in 1873. Major Wingfield originally called the game *sphairistike,* a Greek word that means "playing ball." This name was soon replaced by "lawn tennis," because the game was played on grass courts in England. Tennis replaced croquet as England's most popular outdoor sport.

Quick Notes

- **Martina was named the Female Athlete of the Decade for the 1980s by the Associated Press and United Press International.**

- **Martina was made a member of the International Women's Sports Hall of Fame in 1984.**

- **In 1982, Martina won ninety out of the ninety-three matches she played.**

- **Martina became a United States citizen in 1981.**

- **Martina's serve is so powerful that her ball flies over the net at 90 miles (150 kilometers) an hour.**

Accomplishments

Martina loved living in the United States: "It was the first time in my life when I didn't have to get permission to do anything." Martina was earning a lot of money from playing tennis. She went on shopping sprees, spending thousands of dollars on gold jewelry and clothes. Despite her new freedom, Martina was very lonely. She missed her family and friends in Czechoslovakia.

Feeling depressed, Martina went on eating binges of her favorite new foods, hamburgers and pizza. She did not practice very much and began to rely on her talent instead of hard work to play well.

This changed in 1976 after Martina lost her first match at the U.S. Open. Martina was expected to win the match, but a little-known newcomer won instead. Martina was stunned by the loss. She sat down on the side of the court and cried. Martina knew she needed help if she was going to win again.

Once Martina got in shape and dedicated herself to tennis, she became the world's best woman player.

Later that year, Martina met Sandy Haynie, a **professional** golfer. She became Martina's agent and best friend. Sandy got Martina to exercise, work hard, and stop her bad eating habits.

The hard work paid off. In 1978, Martina was back in top form, and she started to win important tournaments. She won in France at the French Open. Then she won in England at Wimbledon. With these big wins, Martina was ranked the number-one women's tennis player in the world.

Martina rarely left this number-one position over the next **decade**. She dominated women's tennis during the 1980s. In 1984, Martina won the Grand Slam in the world of tennis. To win the Grand Slam, a tennis player must win the world's four major tennis tournaments in a row. These four are: Wimbledon, the French Open, the Australian Open, and the U.S. Open. It is something few professional tennis players accomplish. Martina later won each of these tournaments individually number of times.

Martina retired from professional tennis in 1994. She continues to play in exhibition games and team tennis. Martina Navratilova is considered by many people to be the best woman tennis player in the entire history of the sport.

BACKGROUNDER

Wimbledon

When people started playing tennis in England, the All England Croquet Club changed its name to the All England Croquet and Lawn Tennis Club. In 1877, it sponsored its first major tennis tournament, played in a suburb of London, called Wimbledon. This tournament quickly became thought of as the most important one of the year. Although it is not official, the Wimbledon tournament is considered the world championship of tennis.

Martina won the Wimbledon Championship a record nine times.

"The triumph can't be had without the struggle. And I know what struggle is."

Wilma Rudolph

American Sprinter

Early Years

W hen Wilma was born, she was so tiny that her doctors thought she might die. Later, as a child she came down with one sickness after another, including polio and scarlet fever.

Even though her illness left her with a paralyzed leg and her doctor told her she would never walk again, Wilma was a cheerful and energetic child. She loved to play and wanted to keep right on playing. Instead of running, she hopped. When she had trouble getting around, one of her many brothers and sisters helped her. The whole family took turns **massaging** Wilma's leg four times a day to help make it strong. Every week, Wilma and her mother took the bus to the nearest town, Nashville, Tennessee, to take Wilma to a treatment center.

When Wilma was six, her leg was strong enough for a steel brace. The brace was heavy and awkward, but Wilma was thrilled. Now she could walk on her own, and she was finally allowed to attend school.

BACKGROUNDER

Polio

Polio is a disease that can cause paralysis, leaving its victims unable to walk. It is caused by a virus that attacks the brain and spinal cord. It is often called "infantile paralysis" because scientists once thought that only children caught it. In fact, it can affect a person of any age.
In 1955, Dr. Jonas Salk developed a **vaccine** to protect people from polio.

Before Dr. Jonas Salk developed a vaccine against polio, the disease could paralyze people for life.

Developing Skills

After a few years of wearing the brace, Wilma found she could take it off for short periods and practice walking without it. By the time she was twelve, Wilma was walking, running, and even playing basketball. All without a brace! This was the girl some doctors said would never walk.

Once Wilma started moving freely, she did not stop. She made the basketball team when she was thirteen. She also joined the track team. Wilma was nicknamed Skeeter because she was always buzzing around "like a mosquito," her coach said. Wilma was a great basketball player. She was an even better track athlete. During her first year on the track team, she entered twenty races. She won every one.

"People were going to start separating me from that brace, start thinking of me differently, start saying that Wilma is a healthy kid, just like the rest of them."

Wilma became a track star from the moment she ran her first race.

With Wilma's help, her basketball team went to the Tennessee State Championships. Even though her team lost, Wilma stood out as a great player. The referee, who was also the coach for the track-and-field team at Tennessee State University, noticed that Wilma was a strong runner. He invited her to come to a summer camp for runners.

Her parents were worried, but they let Wilma go. Wilma learned that she had to work hard and "that there was more to winning than just running fast." The hard work paid off. Wilma went to the National **Amateur** Athletic Union meet at the end of the summer. She won all nine races that she entered.

Because of her success at this meet, Wilma went to the trials for the 1956 Olympic Games. She was chosen to go to Melbourne, Australia, where the Games were being held. It was Wilma's first time on an airplane. She did not win the 200-meter event, but she helped her team win a bronze medal in the relay. This was only a small taste of what Wilma could do. She decided right then that she wanted to win more medals. "Gold ones," she said.

> "I've always been positive no matter what happened."

BACKGROUNDER
Track and Field

Track events are those that involve races over various distances. These include running, hurdle, steeplechase, walking, and relays. Field events involve jumping and throwing. The jumps are long jump, triple jump, high jump, and pole vault. The throwing events are the discus, hammer, javelin, and shot-put. Track-and-field events are considered the second most popular sports in the world. The first is soccer. The earliest known track-and-field events were held at the Olympic Games in Ancient Greece. The first recorded contest was in 776 B.C.

The 1956 Tennessee State University relay team. Wilma is second from the right.

BACKGROUNDER

Life after the Olympics

In 1961, Wilma married William Ward. They divorced in 1976. Wilma later married Robert Eldridge, a childhood sweetheart she had known since second grade. After teaching and coaching for many years in Tennessee, Wilma moved with her family to Indiana. She became the director of the Wilma Rudolph Foundation. It gave opportunities to boys and girls to compete in sports.

Accomplishments

I n 1958, Wilma entered Tennessee State University. She became a member of its famous track team called the Tigerbelles. To help pay for her education, she joined the work-aid program. Wilma and other Tigerbelles worked two hours a day, five days a week, at a variety of jobs around the campus.

When Wilma went to the Olympic trials in 1960, she **qualified** for three events. They were the 100 meter, 200 meter, and 4 x 100 team relay. Wilma was off to the Olympic Games in Rome, Italy.

These Games were the first shown on television. Wilma knew that millions of people from around the world would be watching. She was very nervous. To make things worse, Wilma sprained her ankle the day she arrived in Rome.

"The most important aspect is to be yourself and have confidence in yourself."

Wilma's sprained ankle did not stop her from winning three Olympic gold medals in 1960.

When Wilma came to race in the 100-meter event, she forgot about the pain in her ankle. She had come to Rome to win a gold medal, and she was determined to do so. Although she was not the first off the starting block, she was definitely the first across the finish line. Wilma repeated this performance in the 200-meter event. Wilma had won two gold medals.

Wilma had a couple of days to rest before the relay race. For the relay, Wilma was to run in the anchor position. She would run last, and she would be the person to cross the finish line. During the race, the first three runners on Wilma's team all ran in first place. Everything was perfect until the baton was handed to Wilma. The pass was not smooth, and Wilma almost dropped the baton. She had to scramble to catch it.

Because of this accident, Wilma started her part of the race in third place. She had to make up time if she wanted her team to win. Wilma seemed to run faster than ever. At the very last moment, she passed the only runner in front of her and crossed the finish line first. The team came away with a gold medal. Wilma was the first American woman to win three gold medals at a single Olympic Games.

After the Games, Wilma finished her bachelor's degree in education. She became an elementary school teacher, a coach, gave lectures across the United States, and founded the Wilma Rudolph Foundation to help young athletes. In 1994, Wilma died of a brain tumor.

Quick Notes

- In 1977, Wilma wrote the book *Wilma: The Story of Wilma Rudolph*. It was made into a television movie.

- Wilma was a United States Goodwill Ambassador to French West Africa.

- Wilma was a member of the U.S. Olympic Committee.

- Wilma had four children: Yolanda, Djuana, Xurry, and Robert, Jr.

- In 1997, the governor of Tennessee proclaimed June 23, Wilma's birthday, to be Wilma Rudolph Day.

"That one accomplishment—what happened in 1960—nobody can take from me. It was something I worked for. It wasn't something somebody handed me."

"I knew what I wanted to be when I grew up. My goal was to be the greatest athlete that ever lived."

Mildred "Babe" Didrikson Zaharias

American Track Athlete and Golfer

Early Years

Mildred Ella Didrikson loved sports. She was active in sports almost before she learned how to walk! The sixth of seven children, her nickname was Baby. The name was later shortened to Babe after the famous baseball player Babe Ruth. This was after she hit seven home runs in a single baseball game.

From the beginning, Babe outran, outhit, outshot, and outplayed most of the other kids. She owned all the marbles in the neighborhood because she always won. "I had an urge to be first in everything," Babe said.

Babe's talents were not limited to sports. She taught herself to play the harmonica. Like everything she did, she did it well, so well that she started performing on the radio when she was seven years old. She played on a regular program until she was ten.

BACKGROUNDER

Babe's Family

Babe was born in the United States, but her parents were from Norway. Her mother, Hannah, was a champion skater and skier. Her father, Ole, had been a sailor before he moved to the United States. He sailed from Norway to the southern tip of South America seventeen times. Ole loved to tell his children about his sailing trips. Once, when his ship broke up in a storm, he held onto a mast rope for hours to keep from drowning.

Mildred excelled at every sport she tried.

Developing Skills

A s a teenager, Babe took part in all the sports she could: tennis, bowling, track, basketball, diving, baseball, and more. You name it, Babe played it. After she joined her high school basketball team, it did not lose a game.

Because of her great basketball skills, Babe was given a job by an insurance company in Dallas, Texas, simply so she could play on the company's team. This was before she had even finished high school! Babe's parents did not want her to leave school to work, but she convinced them that she could do both. Her family needed the money. It was a lot to do, but Babe got it all done. She went to practices, played games, did her schoolwork, and worked full time as a secretary.

After she graduated from school, Babe stayed on with the company and led its basketball team to the U.S. National **Tournament** three years in a row.

As well as playing basketball for her company, Babe joined its swimming, diving, and track teams. She was actually the company's entire track team! Within a year, she was the best woman track athlete in Texas. Babe had dreamed about going to the Olympics for years. She thought she could do it with track. She convinced the company to send her to the Olympic trials in 1932.

"I never wished for something, I went to work to get it."

Babe represented her company at the Olympic trials.

When Babe marched into the stadium by herself, all the people in the stands began to laugh. How could a "team" of one girl compete against teams of over twenty? These people did not know Babe. She was so angry that she turned around and walked out of the stadium. She was more determined than ever.

Babe showed those stands of people what she could do. There were ten events and Babe entered eight of them. She could not enter the other two because they were at the same time as others. She rushed from one event to the next. To everyone's surprise, Babe won five of the eight events, setting new world records in three of them. She placed first overall, and earned nearly twice as many points as the team of twenty-two that had marched into the stadium ahead of her.

BACKGROUNDER

Young Working Girl

Babe did more than play sports while she was still at high school. Her family did not have much money. To help out, Babe worked in a fig-packing plant, peeling and cleaning figs. Later, Babe found a job sewing potato sacks. She earned a penny for each sack. Babe was so fast that she could make up to sixty-eight cents an hour. Babe kept only a nickel or dime for herself and gave the rest to her mother.

Babe set a world record in the javelin throw.

Accomplishments

George Zaharias

Babe met George when she entered a men's golf tournament. It was love at first sight. The two were married within the year. George had been a professional wrestler, but he gave up his career to become Babe's manager and coach. He was devoted to Babe. He called her "Romance." George even slept in another room the night before Babe's tournaments. He did not want to keep her awake with his snoring. Later, when Babe had cancer and had to stay in hospital, George was constantly at her side, giving her the support she needed.

In 1932, Babe was off to the Olympics. In those days, athletes were allowed to enter only three events. Babe was not happy about this, but she entered the 80-meter hurdles, the javelin throw, and the high jump.

Babe won two gold medals and set new Olympic and world records for both the 80-meter hurdles and the javelin throw. She won a silver medal in the high jump. She had in fact placed first, but because she went over the bar with her head first, rather than her feet, she was bumped to second place. Babe thought this was unfair because that was how she had always jumped.

After the Olympics, there was not much money to be made as a **professional** track athlete. Babe decided to try golf. Golf did not come so easily to Babe as other sports. She had to work hard. She played six days a week, starting at 5:00 A.M. and often practicing sixteen hours a day. Many days, she hit more than 1,500 balls. Her hands would often be blistered and bleeding. Babe just taped them up and kept on hitting golf balls. In 1935, she entered and won the Texas Women's **Amateur** Golf Championship.

"I don't know who my opponents are and, anyways, it wouldn't make a difference."

Babe loved golf, and she loved the attention she received from playing it. She often joked with the other players and the crowd: "Don't you men wish you could hit a ball like that? And me just a little old gal!"

Babe's success brought a lot of attention to women in golf. Before, the game had mainly been played in a gentle way by wealthy women. But Babe was aggressive, and she played to win.

Babe was soon winning tournaments across the United States. During 1947, she won seventeen **consecutive** tournaments. Male or female, no one had ever won so many in a row. One of those tournaments was the British Women's Amateur title. Babe was the first American woman to win it.

In the midst of Babe's golf victories, she was stricken with cancer. She continued to win tournaments, even after having major surgery. In the end, her sickness was one battle Babe could not win. She died in 1956. Today, many people consider her the best female athlete in history.

Quick Notes

- Babe's father built a gymnasium in their backyard. It included a weightlifting machine and bars for high jumping.

- With her earnings from golf, Babe built her dream home in Florida. It was at the end of a golf course, overlooking a small lake. Babe called her house Rainbow Manor.

- The Associated Press voted Babe "Woman Athlete of the Year" five times. It also named her the "Greatest Female Athlete of the First Half of the Twentieth Century."

"She was a golden person … the most splendid woman athlete of all time."

author Paul Gallico

Golf was the last sport Babe mastered.

More Women in Profile

There are thousands of women athletes around the world. The following pages list a few more whom you might want to learn more about on your own. The Suggested Reading list will give you further information on other great women athletes.

1969–

Myriam Bedard
Canadian Biathlete

The biathlon is a combination of cross-country skiing and shooting. In competitions, biathletes ski certain distances, stopping along the way at shooting ranges to fire shots at a target. It is a sport at which Canadian skier, Myriam Bedard, excels. Myriam was introduced to the biathlon when she was fifteen. She already could shoot well because of her training as a **cadet**. When three male cadets needed a woman to join their biathalon team, they asked Myriam. She went on to win a bronze medal at the 1992 Olympic Games in Albertville, France, and two gold medals at the 1994 Olympics in Lillehammer, Norway.

1968–

Hassiba Boulmerka
Algerian Middle-distance Runner

Born in Algeria, Hassiba won a gold medal at the Olympic Games in 1992 in the 1,500-meter race. While most athletes receive tremendous support from their country, Hassiba received death threats. Some people objected to a **Muslim** woman racing in track and field and expected Hassiba to cover herself in public. Hassiba wore shorts and a sleeveless top during her race. Some Muslims accused her of "running with naked legs in front of thousands of men." Hassiba replied that she was an athlete and had to dress properly for competitions.

Hassiba Boulmerka

1907–
Ilona Schacherer Elek
Hungarian Fencer

Ilona was one of the early women champions of the sport of fencing. Her success came fairly late in life. Twice, she was the oldest woman gold medalist at the Olympic Games. She was twenty-nine when she won the gold at the 1936 Games in Berlin, Germany. The next Olympic Games were postponed because of World War II. When they were held again in London, England, in 1948, Ilona again won the gold medal. She went on to compete in the Olympic Games in Helsinki, Finland, in 1952. Although she was forty-five years old, she won the silver medal.

1958–
Kornelia Ender
German Swimmer

Kornelia was thirteen years old when she won three silver medals for Germany at the 1972 Olympic Games. This was only the start for Kornelia. By fourteen, she was the world's fastest swimmer. Within three years of her Olympic victories, Kornelia broke her own world record in the 100-meter freestyle event eight times. By 1976, she had set fifteen world records in swimming. It was no surprise that in 1976, Kornelia became the first woman ever to win four Olympic gold medals at a single Olympic Games.

Fu Mingxia

1979–
Fu Mingxia
Chinese Diver

It is common to see girls in their early teens winning championships in gymnastics and figure skating. Diving was often a sport for older **competitors**—until Fu Mingxia stepped onto the diving board. The Chinese diver made her first appearance at the Olympic Games when she was only thirteen years old. Fu Mingxia proved herself to be a daring and graceful diver. She walked away from the 1992 Olympic Games in Barcelona, Spain, with a gold medal. In 1996, at the Olympic Games in Atlanta, Mingxia won her second gold medal in the women's platform, and she added another gold in the women's springboard. She became the second woman to win both diving events at a single Olympics.

Silken Laumann

1962–

Jackie Joyner-Kersee

American Heptathlete

In 1992, the American athlete Jackie Joyner-Kersee confirmed what many people already thought. She was the world's greatest female athlete. Jackie had just won her second Olympic gold medal in the heptathlon. The heptathlon is a two-day contest in which women compete in seven track-and-field events. They are: the 100-meter hurdles, shotput, high jump, 200-meter run, long jump, javelin throw, and an 800-meter run. In 1988, when she won her first heptathlon, Jackie was named Outstanding Athlete of the Year by *Sporting News*. Only male athletes had been honored with the title before Jackie.

1963–

Julie Krone

American Jockey

Born in the United States, Julie scrambled onto her first pony when she was only three years old. Today, she is considered the most successful woman jockey in the history of thoroughbred horse racing. In horse racing, men and women compete directly with one another, though most jockeys are men. Julie has ridden to more than 2,500 victories and has accumulated nearly $50 million in earnings.

1965–

Silken Laumann

Canadian Rower

In 1991, Canadian-born Silken Laumann was considered the best women's rower in the world. That year, she won the World Cup Championship and the World Championship. Silken was training for the 1992 Olympic Games with high hopes for a gold medal. Two months before the Games, her boat was rammed and Silken suffered a broken ankle and tore a muscle in her lower leg. This did not stop Silken. She went to the Games despite her injury and came away with the bronze medal. Her courage inspired many people. Her coach, Mike Spracklen, said, "Winning isn't always about finishing first, is it? Sometimes it's about conquering yourself." Silken retired from rowing after she won a silver medal at the 1996 Olympics in Atlanta.

1962–

Paula Newby-Fraser

South African Triathlete

Born in Zimbabwe, Paula moved with her family to South Africa when she was four years old. She watched her first Ironman triathlon in 1984, but she never thought she would compete in such a grueling event. An Ironman triathlon involves a 2.4-mile (4000-meter) swim, a 112-mile (180-kilometer) bicycle ride, and a full 26.2-mile (42-kilometer) run. Before long, Paula was training for this event, and within a year, she won her first competition. With this win, Paula was **eligible** to compete in the Ironman in Hawaii. She came in third on her first try. Over the next few years, Paula was always in the winner's circle. She won a total of eight Ironman triathlon world championships and was the first woman to complete the event in less than nine hours.

1973–

Manon Rheaume

Canadian Hockey Goalie

Born in Canada, Manon began skating when she was three years old on the rink her father built in the backyard. Both of Manon's brothers played hockey. When they wanted to practice, they covered Manon with padding, put her in goal, and shot pucks at her. When the goalie could not play for one of her brothers' hockey **tournaments**, Manon filled in. She was only five years old. From then on, she played hockey with boys. In 1992, in Tampa Bay, Florida, Manon became the first woman ever to play in the National Hockey League. Manon now plays for the Canadian National Women's Hockey Team. In 1998, she helped the Canadian Olympic Hockey Team win a silver medal at the Olympic Games in Nagano, Japan.

Manon Rheaume

Glossary

amateur: a person who does something for enjoyment, not money

apparatus: equipment used for a particular purpose, such as gymnastics

cadet: a young person being trained for service in the army, navy, air force, or police force

communist: describes a system in which the state controls all property and methods of production

competitor: a person who takes part in an event in the hope of winning it

consecutive: following one after the other without a break

credited: said to have done something

decade: a ten-year period

defect: to leave one's country illegally

eligible: having all the necessary qualifications

international: having to do with more than one country

massaging: rubbing someone's muscles and joints to relax the body and help the blood circulate

Muslim: a person who practices the Islamic religion

Olympic team: the group of athletes chosen by each country to compete in the Olympic Games

professional: a person who makes money from doing something that other people do for fun

qualify: to be good enough to be chosen for something

status: someone's position or rank

tournament: contest between two or more people or teams

vaccine: a preparation used to protect someone from a disease

Suggested Reading

Breitenbucher, Cathy. *Bonnie Blair: Golden Streak*. Minnesota: Lerner Publications, 1994.

Condon, Robert J. *Great Women Athletes of the Twentieth Century*. Jefferson, North Carolina: McFarland, 1991.

Daly, Wendy. *Bonnie Blair: Power on Ice*. New York: Random House, 1996.

Knudson, Rozanne R. *Martina Navratilova: Tennis Power*. New York: Viking Penguin, 1986.

Krull, Kathleen. *Lives of the Athletes: Thrills and Spills*. Orlando: Harcourt Brace, 1997.

Krull, Kathleen. *Wilma Unlimited: How Wilma Rudolph Became the World's Fastest Woman*. Orlando: Harcourt Brace, 1996.

Lacklan, Carli. *Golden Girls*. New York: McGraw-Hill, 1980.

Layden, Joe. *Women in Sports: The Complete Book on the World's Greatest Female Athletes*. Santa Monica: General Publishing, 1997.

Leder, Jane Mersky. *Martina Navratilova*. Mankato, Minnesota: Crestwood House, 1985.

Long, Wendy. *Celebrating Excellence: Canadian Women Athletes*. Vancouver: Polestar, 1995.

Lynn, Elizabeth A. *Babe Didrikson Zaharias*. Chelsea House, 1989.

Markel, Robert, Nancy Brooks, and Susan Markel. *For the Record: Women in Sports*. New York: World Almanac Publications, 1985.

Saari, Peggy, ed. *Prominent Women of the 20th Century*. Detroit: UXL, 1996.

Index

1 2 3 4 5 6 7 8 9 0 Printed in Canada 8 7 6 5 4 3 2 1 0 9